Grammar Dictionary

by Mary Mason

Illustrated by Iqbal Aslam

Cover by Trevor Carter

LOAN

© 1998 The Questions Publishing Company Ltd
27 Frederick Street, Hockley, Birmingham B1 3HH

ISBN 1-898149-81-X

Design by Antony Johnsto

Printed in Great Britain

Questions Publisł Birmingham

i

What is grammar?

Language is made up of **words** and **grammar**. Words on their own are not much use.

We can compare them with the parts of a car. The wheels, the crankshaft and the windscreen are not much use on their own.

If we know how to put them together we have a car.

And with a car we can go places!

Just as a car is made up of different parts, so language is made up of different kinds of words.

If we know how to put them together we have a meaning.

And with language, we change the world!

The layout of the book

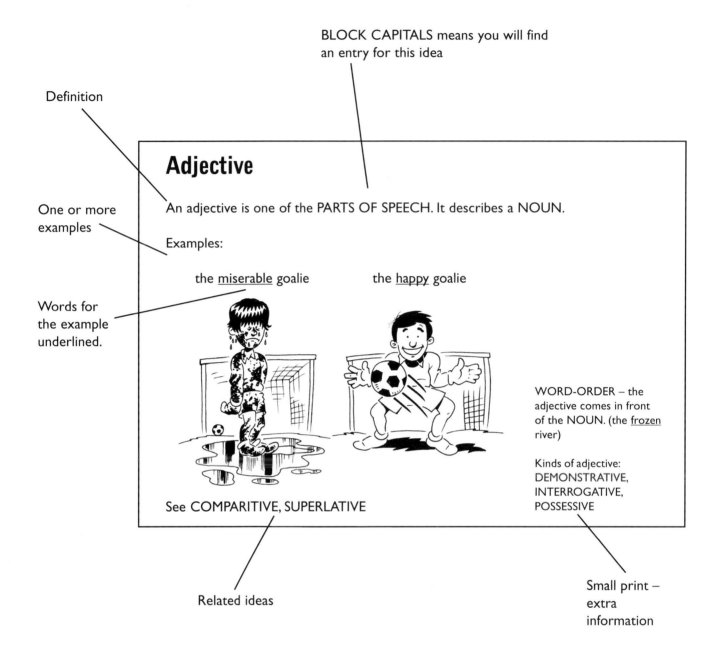

Definition

One or more examples

Words for the example underlined.

BLOCK CAPITALS means you will find an entry for this idea

Adjective

An adjective is one of the PARTS OF SPEECH. It describes a NOUN.

Examples:

the miserable goalie   the happy goalie

WORD-ORDER – the adjective comes in front of the NOUN. (the frozen river)

Kinds of adjective: DEMONSTRATIVE, INTERROGATIVE, POSSESSIVE

See COMPARITIVE, SUPERLATIVE

Related ideas

Small print – extra information

Grammar and punctuation

There are many differences between speech and writing. When we talk we have many ways of making our meaning clear – the ups and downs of our voice, for instance. We lose this when we write. There is a grammatical difference too: we speak in clauses, but we write in sentences.

Punctuation helps the reader through the grammar of the sentence.

Active voice

The VERB is in the active VOICE when the SUBJECT of the CLAUSE does the action.

Examples:

SUBJECT	VERB	OBJECT		SUBJECT	VERB	OBJECT
Phyllis	frightened	the monster		Shazia	lit	the bunsen burner.

See VOICE

Adjective

An adjective is one of the PARTS OF SPEECH. It describes a NOUN.

Examples:

the miserable goalie   the happy goalie

WORD-ORDER
– the adjective comes in front
of the NOUN. (the frozen river)

Kinds of adjective:
DEMONSTRATIVE,
INTERROGATIVE,
POSSESSIVE

See COMPARATIVE, SUPERLATIVE

Adjective clause

An adjective CLAUSE is a clause which acts like an ADJECTIVE. It describes a NOUN.

Example:

This is the bicycle <u>which was squashed by a lorry.</u>

An adjective clause usually begins with a RELATIVE PRONOUN. It is a SUBORDINATE CLAUSE

Adjective phrase

An adjective PHRASE is a group of WORDS which act together as an ADJECTIVE. Together they describe a NOUN.

Example:

the cat <u>on the roof</u>
(*Which cat? The one <u>on the roof</u>.*)

An adjective phrase has two parts:

PREPOSITION   NOUN

on   *the roof*
with   *a drink*

WORD-ORDER:
The adjective phrase comes after the noun.

Adverb

An adverb is one of the PARTS OF SPEECH. It answers questions about the VERB.

Examples:

He found seven baby rabbits <u>there</u>.
(*<u>Where</u> did he find the rabbits? <u>There</u>*.)

Now she lives <u>dangerously</u>.
(*<u>How</u> does she live? <u>Dangerously</u>.*
<u>When</u>? <u>Now</u>.)

WORD-ORDER:

The adverb is often last:
I drew the figure <u>carefully</u>

But it can be first:
<u>Carefully</u> I drew the figure.

And it can be in other places:
I <u>carefully</u> drew the figure

Other kinds of adverb: COMPARATIVE, SUPERLATIVE, INTERROGATIVE, NEGATIVE

Adverb clause

An adverb CLAUSE acts like an ADVERB. It answers questions about the VERB.

Examples:

We were afraid, <u>because the creature was huge.</u>
(*<u>Why</u> were we afraid?*)
<u>When I shouted "Boo!"</u>, it ran away.
(*<u>When</u> did it run away?*)

WORD-ORDER:
An adverb clause can come after the MAIN CLAUSE:
We were afraid, <u>because the creature was huge</u>
Or it can come before the main clause:
<u>When I shouted "Boo!"</u>, it ran away.

An adverb clause is a SUBORDINATE clause.

It begins with a SUBORDINATING CONJUNCTION.

Adverb phrase

An adverb PHRASE is a group of WORDS acting together as an ADVERB.
Like an adverb, it answers questions about the VERB.

Examples:

He found seven baby rabbits <u>in the hutch</u>.
(<u>Where</u> did he find the rabbits? <u>In the hutch</u>.)

WORD-ORDER:
An adverb phrase often comes at the end of a clause:
She packed her bags <u>before breakfast</u>.

But it can come at the beginning:
<u>*Before breakfast*</u> *she packed her bags.*

An adverb phrase has two parts:

PREPOSITION	NOUN
in	*the hutch*
before	*breakfast*

Agreement

If a SUBJECT is SINGULAR, the VERB is also singular. If the subject is PLURAL, the verb is also plural. That is: the subject and verb <u>agree</u>.

Example: Fiona <u>is</u> happy.

Fiona and Ahmed <u>are</u> happy.

A NOUN is followed by a PRONOUN which is the same in GENDER and NUMBER. That is: The noun and pronoun <u>agree</u>.

Samantha hit <u>her</u> thumb with a hammer. <u>She</u> yelled. The workmen finished early and <u>they</u> went home.

Agreement is not very important in English. Languages such as German, French and Spanish have many more rules of agreement.

Apostrophe (1)

We use an apostrophe to show that something belongs to somebody.

Example:

<u>Daisy's</u> tractor

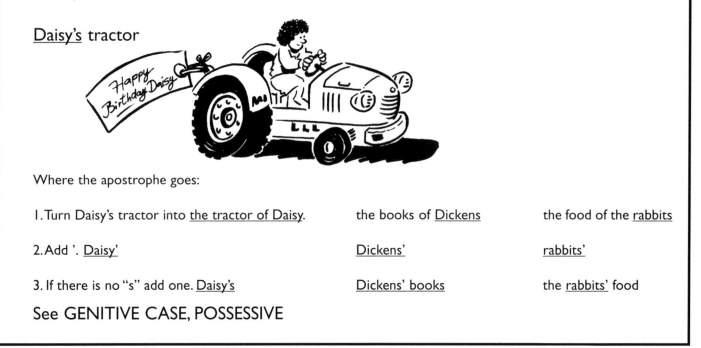

Where the apostrophe goes:

1. Turn Daisy's tractor into <u>the tractor of Daisy</u>.	the books of <u>Dickens</u>	the food of the <u>rabbits</u>
2. Add '. <u>Daisy'</u>	<u>Dickens'</u>	<u>rabbits'</u>
3. If there is no "s" add one. <u>Daisy's</u>	<u>Dickens'</u> books	the <u>rabbits'</u> food

See GENITIVE CASE, POSSESSIVE

Apostrophe (2)

We use an apostrophe to show missing letters.

Examples:
don't (= do not)   couldn't (= could not)   can't (= cannot)
I'm (=I am)   he's (=he is or he has)   they're (=they are)

Apposition

NOUNS are in apposition when they refer to the same person (or thing) in two different ways.

Example:
Mr. Marwa, the teacher of Class 5, never loses his temper.
(*Mr. Marwa and the teacher of Class 5 are the same person. They are <u>in apposition</u>.*)

See COMMA (3)

NOUN CLAUSES can also be in apposition to a noun:

Example:
I stick to my opinion that it was a waste of time.
(<u>*My opinion*</u> *and* <u>*that it was a waste of time*</u> *are the same thing. They are in apposition*)

Article, definite

"The" is the definite article. It is a PART OF SPEECH. It points to a particular person or thing.

Example:
<u>the</u> duck on the nest

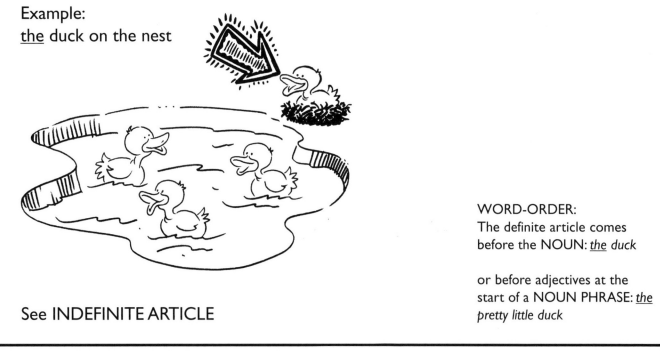

See INDEFINITE ARTICLE

WORD-ORDER:
The definite article comes before the NOUN: <u>*the*</u> *duck*

or before adjectives at the start of a NOUN PHRASE: <u>*the*</u> *pretty little duck*

Article, indefinite

"A" (or "an") is the indefinite article. It is a PART OF SPEECH.

It means any example of the kind.

Example: a little duck (= any little duck)

WORD-ORDER:
The indefinite article comes before the NOUN: *a duck*

or before adjectives at the start of a NOUN PHRASE: *a pretty little duck*

Plurals: There is no plural indefinite article: *ducks, pretty little ducks*

See DEFINITE ARTICLE

Aspect

The aspect of a VERB tells us whether the action is finished or not.

Examples:

Unfinished (IMPERFECT ASPECT)
He <u>was coming</u> down the slide.

Finished (PERFECT ASPECT)
He <u>has come</u> down the slide.

Auxiliary verb

An auxiliary VERB helps the verb form different TENSES and MOODS.

Examples:

Mabel <u>was</u> riding the camel.
Mabel <u>will</u> not ride the camel.
Mabel <u>has</u> ridden the camel.
<u>Did</u> Mabel ride the camel?

The word AUXILIARY comes from the Latin
word *auxilium* – help.

See PAST PARTICIPLE (1), PRESENT PARTICIPLE (1)

Bound morpheme

A bound MORPHEME cannot stand alone.
It has to be joined to a FREE MORPHEME to make a WORD.

Examples:
dis-   re-   -ed   -ly   -ful

A bound morpheme may come at
the beginning of a WORD:
<u>re</u>start   <u>dis</u>agree   <u>un</u>do

Or at the end of a word:
bright<u>est</u>   keep<u>er</u>   think<u>ing</u>
boast<u>ed</u>   goal<u>s</u>   unsuccessful<u>ly</u>

See: FREE MORPHEME, PREFIX, SUFFIX

Brackets   (...)

We use brackets for enclosing extra information without interrupting the flow of the sentence.

Example:

The shark (whose name was Slasher) came speeding towards us.

Sometimes we have a choice between COMMAS and brackets.

Example: The shark, whose name was Slasher, came speeding towards us.

Sometimes we have a choice between brackets and DASHES.

Example: The shark – whose name was Slasher – came speeding towards us.

Capital letters   (1)

We use a capital letter to start a SENTENCE.

Example:

Once upon a time there was a king and a queen. They were very happy except for one thing. They had no children. Then at last they had a little girl, who would one day inherit the kingdom.

See FULL STOP (1)

Capital letters   (2)

We use capital letters for the name of a particular person or place.

Examples:

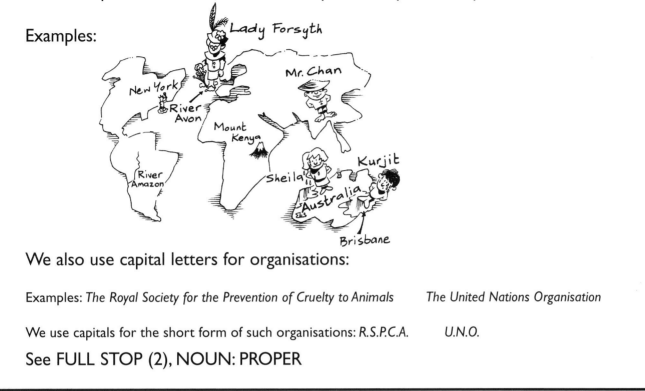

We also use capital letters for organisations:

Examples: *The Royal Society for the Prevention of Cruelty to Animals*   *The United Nations Organisation*

We use capitals for the short form of such organisations: *R.S.P.C.A.*   *U.N.O.*

See FULL STOP (2), NOUN: PROPER

- -

Case

We use CASE when the FORM of a NOUN or PRONOUN shows the work it does in the CLAUSE.

Examples:

SUBJECT	VERB	OBJECT		SUBJECT	VERB	OBJECT
She	washed	the dog.		The dog	washed	her.

Case is not very important in English. It is very important in other languages such as Russian or German.

See: WORD-ORDER, NOMINATIVE, ACCUSATIVE, GENITIVE, DATIVE

Case: accusative

This is the FORM of PRONOUNS which shows they are the OBJECT of the CLAUSE.

Example:

The dog washed <u>her</u>.

After PREPOSITIONS pronouns are in the accusative case:

with <u>me</u>   after <u>him</u>   before <u>her</u>   beside <u>us</u>   on <u>them</u>

See: CASE, WORD-ORDER

Case: dative

This is the FORM of the PRONOUN which shows it is the INDIRECT OBJECT of the CLAUSE.

Example:
We gave <u>him</u> a present.

I gave <u>her</u> a bunch of flowers.
They showed <u>me</u> the computer.
Tell <u>us</u> a story!
We wished <u>them</u> a happy holiday.

These pronouns are exactly the same as pronouns in the ACCUSATIVE CASE

It is the WORD-ORDER which tells us that they are the indirect object. (They come before the DIRECT OBJECT.)

Clause

A clause is the pattern we use for speaking and writing.

The pattern of the clause is:

SUBJECT   VERB   OBJECT   ADVERB

Examples:

He	found	seven baby rabbits	in the hutch
Jim	loves	rabbits	

Kinds of clause:
MAJOR, MINOR, MAIN, SUBORDINATE, ADJECTIVE, ADVERB, NOUN

Colon   (1)   :

We use a colon to introduce a list.

Example:

The children who gained their Swimming Certificates were:

Colon   (2)   :

We use a colon instead of a full stop when we want to show that two sentences are connected – for example, by cause and effect.

Example:

One day Sandra rushed across the road without thinking: the result was a very frightening accident.

Comma   (1)   ,

We use commas to show our reader the grammar within a sentence. This may be to show where two CLAUSES meet.

Example: When everybody is ready, I'll bring in the dinner.

If the sentence is short we have a choice of using a comma or not.

When everybody is ready, I'll bring in the dinner.   or   *When everybody is ready I'll bring in the dinner.*

Comma   (2)   ,

We use commas to mark the items in a list.

Example:

The children who gained their Swimming Certificates were: Jane, Rashid, Ahmed, Germaine and Greta.

Comma   (3)   ,

We use commas to mark the items in APPOSITION.

Example: Mr. Marwa, the teacher of Class 5, never loses his temper.

CLAUSES in apposition are not marked off by commas.

Example: I stick to my opinion <u>that it was a waste of time</u>.

Comma (4) ,

We use a comma to mark off words which say something about the whole sentence.

Example:

First of all, Joan suggested that the creature lived in a burrow. Jitpu, as usual, was sure that his aunt had brought it back from India. Finally, we decided that it must have come from Outer Space. The creature, however, sat there unmoved.

If the sentence is short, we have the choice of using commas or not.

Example: First of all Joan suggested that the creature lived in a burrow.

See SENTENCE ADVERB

Command

When we want somebody to do something, we give a command.

Example:

Don't touch the switch!

The VERB in a command is in the IMPERATIVE MOOD.

In writing, a command ends with an EXCLAMATION MARK. (!)

WORD-ORDER:
A command begins with the verb. There is no SUBJECT.

We can tell the subject is *you* because we may follow the verb with *your*:

Eat your peas!
Wash your neck!
Look after your mouse!

Comparative

The comparative compares one thing or event with another.

Example:

Joe is <u>happier</u> than Rachel.

These kinds of WORDS have a comparative form:

1. ADJECTIVES
a <u>silly</u> song, a <u>sillier</u> song
an <u>interesting</u> game, a <u>more interesting</u> game

2. ADVERBS
He works <u>hard</u>. I work <u>harder</u> than him.
She plays the piano <u>beautifully</u>, but he plays even <u>more beautifully</u>.

See SUPERLATIVE

Complement

A complement is a NOUN which is the same thing as the SUBJECT

Example:

Sharleen is <u>an acrobat</u>.
(*Sharleen and the acrobat are one and the same.*)

A complement is an ADJECTIVE which describes the subject.

Example:

The goalkeeper is <u>happy</u>.
(*"happy" describes the goalie.*)

Complex sentence

A complex SENTENCE has at least one MAIN CLAUSE plus at least one SUBORDINATE CLAUSE.

Example:

Jim had not realised that Floppy was pregnant until he found seven baby rabbits in the hutch.

MAIN CLAUSE	SUBORDINATE CLAUSE (1)	SUBORDINATE CLAUSE (2)
Jim had not realised	that Floppy was pregnant	until he found seven baby rabbits in the hutch

Example: Clauses in complex sentences are joined together by JOINING-WORDS

Compound sentence

A compound sentence consists of two or more SIMPLE SENTENCES joined together by *and* or *but*.

Example:

Simple sentences:

The King and Queen lived in a castle.

They were very happy.

They had no children.

Compound sentence:

The King and Queen lived in a castle <u>and</u> they were very happy <u>but</u> they had no children.

Conjunction

A conjunction is one of the PARTS OF SPEECH. It joins CLAUSES together.

With conjunctions we can make COMPOUND or COMPLEX SENTENCES.

Example:

Jasbinder went to bed <u>but</u> she did not sleep.

Kinds of conjunctions:

1. Co-ordinating: *and or but.* These can join together any bits of language of the same kind:

WORDS: *poor <u>but</u> honest, Arthur <u>or</u> Jim*

PHRASES: *in the wood <u>and</u> by the fountain*

CLAUSES: *Jim fell into the pond <u>and</u> Arthur had to fish him out.*

2. Sub-ordinating: <u>if, that, when, because, although, wherever,</u> etc.

These join together SUBORDINATE CLAUSES.

Dash –

We use a dash to add some extra information without interrupting the flow of the sentence.

Example:
Tina's mother had warned her not to touch the dog – which had a reputation for biting people – but Tina couldn't help herself.

We sometimes have a choice between BRACKETS and dashes.
Example:
Tina's mother had warned her not to touch the dog (which had a reputation for biting people) but Tina couldn't help herself.

Sometimes we have a choice between COMMAS and dashes.
Example:
Tina's mother had warned her not to touch the dog, which had a reputation for biting people, but Tina couldn't help herself.

Declarative mood

The VERB is in the declarative MOOD when we make a STATEMENT.

Examples:

The rats <u>are eating</u> the electric cables.

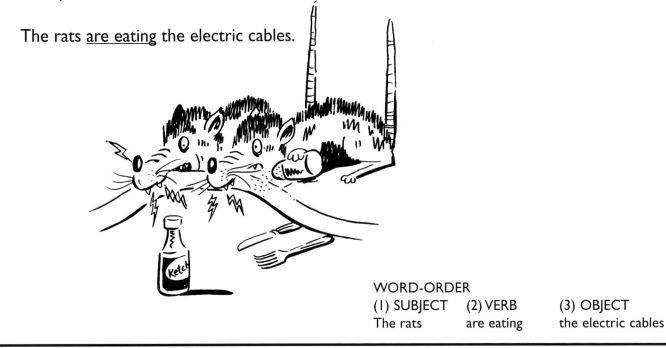

WORD-ORDER
(1) SUBJECT	(2) VERB	(3) OBJECT
The rats	are eating	the electric cables

. . . .

Demonstrative

Demonstrative words tell us if the noun is near to or far from the speaker.

Examples:

<u>this</u> sunflower   <u>that</u> sunflower

There are only four demonstrative words: *this, that, these, those*

Two kinds of words are demonstrative:

ADJECTIVES
<u>*this*</u> *song*   <u>*these*</u> *songs*   <u>*that*</u> *song*   <u>*those*</u> *songs*

PRONOUNS
<u>*This*</u> *is the answer.*   *It's a shame about <u>that</u>. I'd like to see <u>these</u>.*   <u>*Those*</u> *are the wrong ones.*

See: SINGULAR, PLURAL

Dots   ...

We use dots to show we have left something unfinished.

Example:

This is the end of the story for the moment, but some years later Toby was walking along the canal bank and ...

Exclamation mark   !!!   (1)

An exclamation mark shows that the sentence is a COMMAND.

Examples:
Don't touch the switch!

If you hear a noise, hide!
Hide your eyes until I've counted twenty!
Go to bed!

See COMMAND

Exclamation mark !!! (2)

An exclamation mark shows that we have strong feelings about the sentence - delight, horror, surprise etc.

Examples:

Wow!
What a lovely dog!

Finite verb

A finite VERB has a SUBJECT.

Example:

SUBJECT   VERB

Sukvinder   <u>can ride</u> a horse.

No-one   <u>knows</u>.
Someone   <u>is being</u> silly.

A MAJOR CLAUSE has a finite verb.

See: NON-FINITE VERB

Form

We describe the PARTS OF SPEECH according to their form – that is, what they look like.

Examples:

Only NOUNS have a SINGULAR form and a PLURAL form.

frog   frogs

Only VERBS have a PRESENT and PAST TENSE: *play   played*

Only ADJECTIVES and ADVERBS have a COMPARATIVE and a SUPERLATIVE form.
long   longer   longest

Free morpheme

A free morpheme can stand alone as a WORD.

Examples:
bright   goal   keep   play   ball   success

A free morpheme may join with other free morphemes to make more words:
rail-way   match-box   post-box

It may also join with BOUND MORPHEMES to make new words:
bright-est   goal-keep-er   play -ed   ball -s   un-success-ful-ly

Full stop   (1)

A full stop marks the end of a SENTENCE.

Examples:
Once upon a time there was a king and a queen. They were very happy except for one thing. They had no children. Then at last they had a little girl, who would one day inherit the kingdom.

Read your work aloud. The sound will tell you where the sentence ends.

Full stop   (2)

A full stop shows that a word has been shortened.

Examples:

P.T. (Physical Training)

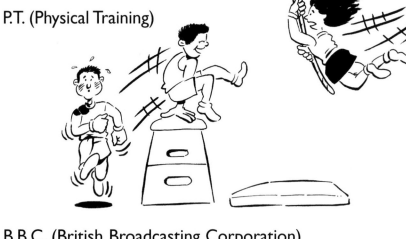

B.B.C. (British Broadcasting Corporation)
P.T.O. (Please Turn Over)
Jan. (January)
Mon. (Monday)

We use a full stop after some Latin words which have been shortened.

Examples:
e.g. (ex exempla)
= for example
etc. (et cetera)
= and other things
i.e. (id est) = that is

Function

The function of a WORD is the work it does in the CLAUSE

Examples:

ADJECTIVES describe nouns.

NOUNS can be SUBJECT or OBJECT.

ADVERBS answer questions about the VERB.

The <u>miserable</u> goalie   the <u>happy</u> goalie

Future tense

VERBS in the future TENSE tell what will happen in the future.

Examples:

Tomorrow I <u>shall go</u> to the seaside.

This time next week they <u>will be enjoying </u>the sunshine in Majorca.
I'm <u>going to finish</u> my homework soon.
Next year the stadium <u>will have been built</u>.

You can check if the verb is in the future tense by adding adverbs like *tomorrow* and *soon*.

The future tenses use the AUXILIARY VERBS *shall* and *will*.

Hyphen   (2) -

We use a hyphen to show that a word which has been split up is all one.

Examples:

We were very <u>sur-</u>
<u>prised</u> to see a <u>rain-</u>
<u>bow</u> so late in
the year.

When we have to split a
word like this, we split it at
the points where it makes
sense.

Not: *We were very surpr-*
ised to see a rainbow so l-
ate in the year.

Imperative mood

The VERB is in the imperative MOOD when we give a COMMAND.

Example:

Don't touch
the switch!

Imperfect aspect

If a VERB is in the imperfect ASPECT, the action is unfinished.

Examples:

He <u>is coming</u> down the slide.

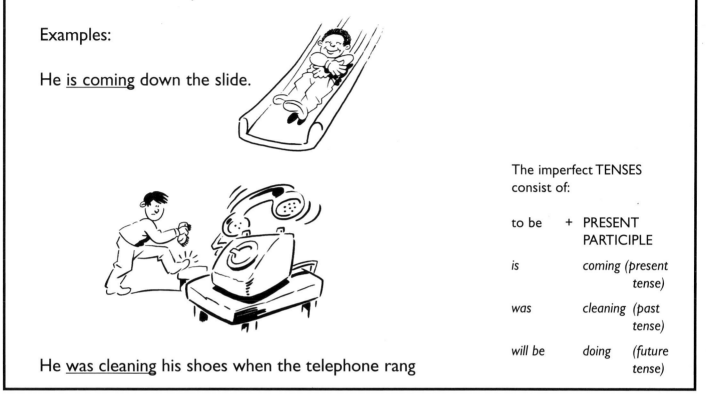

He <u>was cleaning</u> his shoes when the telephone rang

The imperfect TENSES consist of:

to be	+	PRESENT PARTICIPLE
is		*coming (present tense)*
was		*cleaning (past tense)*
will be		*doing (future tense)*

Infinitive

The infinitive is a NON-FINITE VERB. It is the name of the verb.

Examples: to do, to think, to speak, to be

We use the infinitive to form some MINOR CLAUSES.

Example:
We opened the window <u>to get some fresh air</u>.

The infinitive has no SUBJECT. But it may have an OBJECT:
I don't want <u>to do my homework</u>.

It may have ADVERBS:
<u>To go to bed at this time</u> is stupid.

The minor clause may act like a NOUN:
I want <u>to go</u>.
(<u>What</u> do you want?)
or
it may act like an ADVERB:
We swim <u>to keep fit</u>.
(<u>Why</u> do you swim?)

Interjection

An interjection is an exclamation that we throw into the conversation.

Examples:

"<u>Wow</u>! That's amazing!"
"<u>Hurray</u>! We've won the lottery!"
"<u>Oh dear</u>! I can't find the key."

INTERJECTION comes from the Latin words:
jacere - to throw, *inter* - between, among

Interrogative mood

The VERB is in the interrogative mood when we ask a QUESTION.

Example:

Questions like these have the answer: "Yes" or "No".

A question has a QUESTION MARK at the end.

The word INTER-ROGATIVE comes from the Latin *rogare* - to ask, *inter* - between.

Interrogative words

Interrogative words ask QUESTIONS.

Examples:

WORD-ORDER: Interrogative words start the sentence. A sentence which starts with an interrogative word has a QUESTION MARK at the end.

Kinds of interrogative words
PRONOUNS:
<u>What</u> did she say?
<u>Who</u> shall I ask for?
<u>Which</u> do you want to buy?

ADJECTIVES:
<u>Whose</u> book is this?
<u>Which</u> rabbit died?

ADVERBS:
<u>When</u> will you pay me? <u>Where</u> were they?   <u>Why</u> did she leave?

INTERROGATIVE comes from the Latin *rogare* = to ask.

Intransitive verb

An intransitive VERB has no OBJECT.

Examples:

SUBJECT	VERB	OBJECT
The alarm	<u>rang</u>.	

The birds <u>were singing</u>.
It <u>is raining</u>.
I <u>know</u>.
The bride <u>waited</u>.
Albert <u>remembered</u>.

See: TRANSITIVE VERB

Irregular

IRREGULAR WORDS do not follow the most common pattern for their class.

NOUNS: REGULAR nouns form their plural with -s: *frog*   *frog<u>s</u>*

Some irregular nouns are:

child   children

VERBS: Regular verbs form their past tense with -*ed*. play played

Some irregular verbs are:
bring brought
blow blew

mouse   mice
sheep   sheep

Joining-words

These join CLAUSES to make SENTENCES (COMPOUND and COMPLEX).

Example:

The princess, <u>who</u> was very beautiful, had been punished by her father <u>and</u> imprisoned in a tower, <u>because</u> she wanted to marry a woodcutter.

Kinds of joining-words: CONJUNCTIONS and RELATIVE words.

Main clause

Every SENTENCE has at least one main CLAUSE.

Example:

When he looked in the morning, <u>Jim found seven baby rabbits in the hutch</u>.

A main clause can stand on its own as a SIMPLE SENTENCE.

Example: Jim found seven baby rabbits in the hutch.

See: CONJUNCTION, SUBORDINATE CLAUSE, RELATIVE

There may be more than one main clause in a sentence.
Example:
<u>Three of them were black</u>[1] and <u>the others were brown</u>[2].

If a sentence has more than one clause, the others are joined to the main clause by JOINING-WORDS.
Examples:
<u>When</u> they bought her, Floppy was already pregnant.
She gave birth to seven baby rabbits, <u>which</u> were very sweet.

Major clause

A major clause has a SUBJECT and a VERB. (That is: it has a FINITE VERB.)

Example:

SUBJECT	VERB
The owl	hooted.

A major clause may be a MAIN clause:
The owl hooted.

or a SUBORDINATE clause:
We all jumped <u>when the owl hooted</u>.

Kinds of major clause:
MAIN, ADJECTIVE, NOUN ADVERB, SUBORDINATE

Minor clause

A minor clause has a VERB but no SUBJECT.

Example:

We love <u>dancing</u>.

A minor clause may act like an ADJECTIVE: The man <u>wearing a bowler hat</u> must be very hot. (<u>Which</u> man?)

Or it may act like an ADVERB: Stir the porridge <u>to prevent it from sticking</u>. (<u>Why</u> should I stir the pot?)

Or it may act like a NOUN: I want <u>to be an acrobat</u>, when I am older. (<u>What</u> do you want?)

See: GERUND, INFINITIVE, PRESENT PARTICIPLE, PAST PARTICIPLE

Modal verb

Modal verbs tell us whether how likely or important it is that something will happen.

Example: She <u>can</u> play the trumpet but she <u>won't</u>.

Mood

Each VERB has a choice of MOOD:

DECLARATIVE: Used for STATEMENTS.
The rats <u>are eating</u> the electric cables.

INTERROGATIVE: Used for QUESTIONS.

IMPERATIVE: Used for COMMANDS.
<u>Don't touch</u> the switch!

Morpheme

A morpheme is the smallest piece of language which has a meaning.

Examples:
tough - est   goal - keep - er

Morphemes combine
to make WORDS.
the   toughest   goalkeeper

See: BOUND MORPHEME and FREE MORPHEME

Negative verbs

Positive VERBS tell us what happens. Negative verbs tell us what does not happen.

Example:

I did<u>n't</u> know that.   The hamster is <u>not</u> well.
Do<u>n't</u> you believe me?

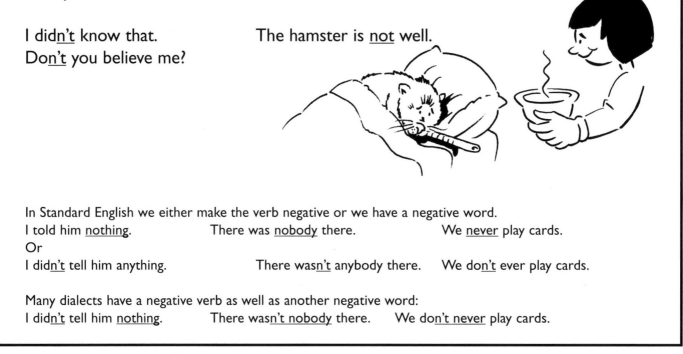

In Standard English we either make the verb negative or we have a negative word.
I told him <u>nothing</u>.   There was <u>nobody</u> there.   We <u>never</u> play cards.
Or
I did<u>n't</u> tell him anything.   There was<u>n't</u> anybody there.   We do<u>n't</u> ever play cards.

Many dialects have a negative verb as well as another negative word:
I did<u>n't</u> tell him <u>nothing</u>.   There was<u>n't</u> nobody there.   We do<u>n't</u> never play cards.

Negative words

Negative words tell us what does not happen.

Example:

We *never* saw it.   I've got *nothing* in my pockets.
He got no reply.
Nobody knows.

Kinds of negative WORDS

PRONOUNS: nobody nothing   none

ADJECTIVES: <u>no</u> money

ADVERBS: nowhere   never

Nominalisation

When we change an ADJECTIVE or a VERB into a NOUN, we call it nominalisation.

Examples:

Long (adjective)

The snake was very <u>long</u>.

<u>Length</u> (noun)

We measured its <u>length</u>.

to create (verb)

She <u>created</u> a model train

<u>creation</u> (noun)

Her brothers loved her <u>creation</u>

See NOUN: ABSTRACT

. . . .

Nominative case

This is the form of PRONOUNS which shows they are the SUBJECT of the CLAUSE.

Example:

<u>She</u> washed the dog.

NOUNS do not do not have a special FORM when they are the subject in English (i.e. have a nominative case). In some languages they do - German, Russian etc.

See: CASE, WORD-ORDER

Non-finite verb

This is a VERB without a SUBJECT.

Examples:

<u>Squashed</u> by a lorry, the bicycle was useless.
<u>Singing</u> sweetly, the canary did not see the cat.
<u>Skating</u> is their favourite sport.
<u>To fly</u> is what we want.
<u>To live</u> we must eat.

We love <u>dancing.</u>

Kinds of non-finite verbs:
PRESENT PARTICIPLE,
PAST PARTICIPLE,
GERUND, INFINITIVE

MINOR CLAUSES have
non-finite verbs.

. . . .

Noun

A noun is one of the PARTS OF SPEECH. It names things in the world.

Examples:

goalpost   ball   goalkeeper

How we can tell that a word is a noun

A noun can have <u>the</u> in front of it.
<u>the</u> goalpost   <u>the</u> ball   <u>the</u> goalkeeper

A noun can be SINGULAR or PLURAL.
Singular: *goalpost*   *ball*   *goalkeeper*
Plural: *goalposts*   *balls*   *goalkeepers*

Noun: abstract

An abstract noun names an idea.

Examples:

<u>happiness</u>   <u>gravity</u>   <u>hope</u>   <u>pain</u>

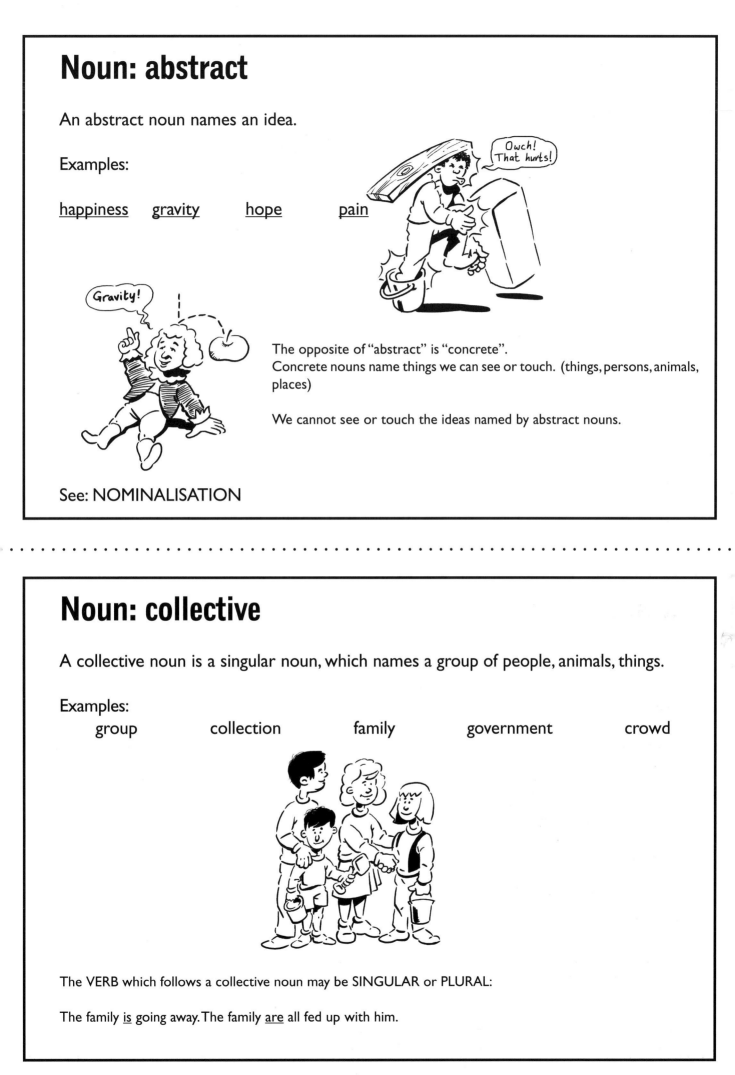

The opposite of "abstract" is "concrete".
Concrete nouns name things we can see or touch. (things, persons, animals, places)

We cannot see or touch the ideas named by abstract nouns.

See: NOMINALISATION

Noun: collective

A collective noun is a singular noun, which names a group of people, animals, things.

Examples:
group   collection   family   government   crowd

The VERB which follows a collective noun may be SINGULAR or PLURAL:

The family <u>is</u> going away. The family <u>are</u> all fed up with him.

Noun: common

A common noun names people and things which there are many examples of.

Examples:

table

teacher

canary

monster

Noun: proper

A proper noun names a particular person or place.

Examples:

Jessica

Paris

Australia

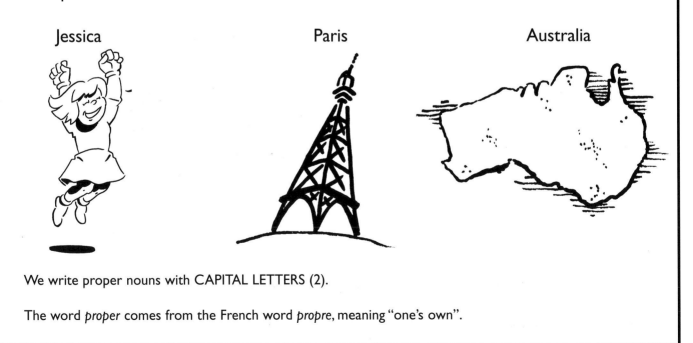

We write proper nouns with CAPITAL LETTERS (2).

The word *proper* comes from the French word *propre*, meaning "one's own".

Noun clause

A noun CLAUSE does the work of a NOUN.

Example: Jasbinder said <u>that she was fed up</u>.

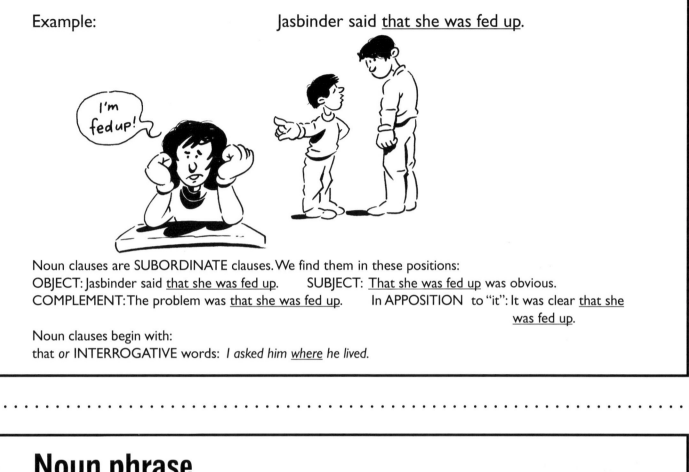

Noun clauses are SUBORDINATE clauses. We find them in these positions:

OBJECT: Jasbinder said <u>that she was fed up</u>.   SUBJECT: <u>That she was fed up</u> was obvious.

COMPLEMENT: The problem was <u>that she was fed up</u>.   In APPOSITION to "it": It was clear <u>that she was fed up</u>.

Noun clauses begin with:

that *or* INTERROGATIVE words: *I asked him <u>where</u> he lived.*

Noun phrase

A noun PHRASE is a group of WORDS which work together as a NOUN.

Example:

<u>The crazy old goalkeeper with the big white beard</u> saved the day!

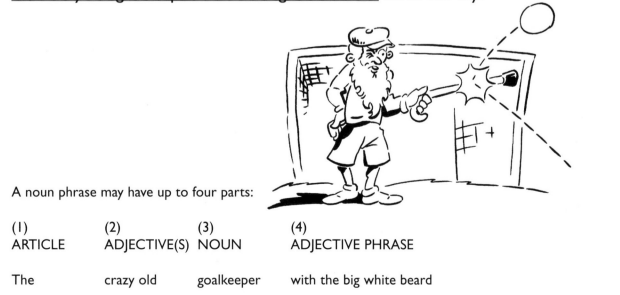

A noun phrase may have up to four parts:

(1) ARTICLE	(2) ADJECTIVE(S)	(3) NOUN	(4) ADJECTIVE PHRASE
The	crazy old	goalkeeper	with the big white beard

Number

The choice of SINGULAR or PLURAL is called number.

Examples:

The <u>ball</u> hit <u>him</u>. (singular)

The <u>balls</u> hit <u>them</u>. (plural)

In English only NOUNS and PRONOUNS are singular or plural.

See REGULAR, IRREGULAR

Object: direct

A direct object tells us who or what the VERB happened to.

Example:

The dog washed <u>Jane</u>

See ACCUSATIVE CASE

WORD-ORDER:
The direct object comes after the VERB.

What can be the object:
NOUN: *He lost <u>the ball</u>.*
PRONOUN: *Shaheen beat <u>me</u>.*
NOUN PHRASE: *He found <u>seven baby rabbits</u>.*
NOUN CLAUSE: *He told me <u>that he had lost the ball</u>.*

Object: indirect

An indirect object is the person who gets the direct object.

Example:

We gave <u>Ahmed</u> a present.

See DATIVE CASE

Very few VERBS are followed by an indirect object: to give, to send, to wish etc.

Kinds of WORDS which can be indirect object:

NOUN: I sent <u>my friend</u> a postcard.

PRONOUN: Shaheen told <u>me</u> a story.

NOUN PHRASE: Jim told <u>the girl with red hair</u> that he loved her.

WORD-ORDER: The indirect object comes before the direct object.

Part of speech

A part of speech is a kind of WORD. Each part of speech has its own FORM and FUNCTION.

Examples:

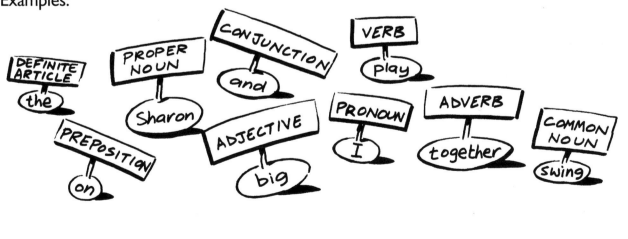

Sharon and I play together on the big swing.

Sometimes we use the name *word-class* instead of part of speech.

See: NOUN, VERB, ADJECTIVE, ADVERB, PRONOUN, PREPOSITION, ARTICLE

Participle

Participles are NON-FINITE VERBS. They can be used as ADJECTIVES.

Examples:

<u>running</u> shoes   <u>parking</u> ticket   <u>painted</u> nails   <u>knitted</u> jumpers   <u>frozen</u> food

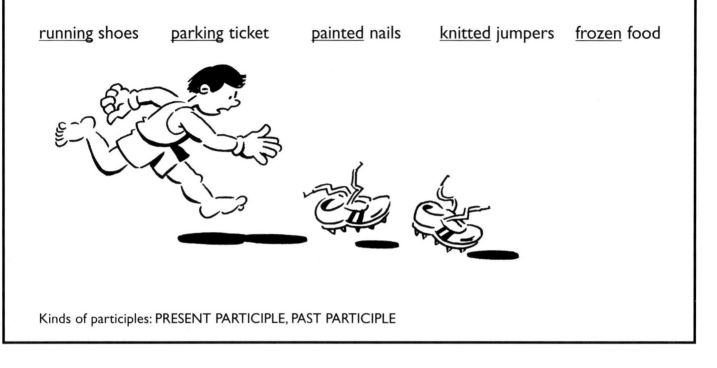

Kinds of participles: PRESENT PARTICIPLE, PAST PARTICIPLE

Particle

Particles are the same WORDS as PREPOSITIONS.

Examples: off   down   on   out   under

They are particles when they change the meaning of VERBS

Examples:
I turned the mattress.
He turned <u>down</u> the offer of a job. (= refused)
The animal turned <u>on</u> me. (= attacked)
It all turned <u>out</u> quite well in the end.
(= happened)
The spider in my soup turned me <u>off</u>.
(= made me dislike it)

       Grammar Dictionary

Passive voice

When the VERB is passive, we focus on the action rather than who is doing it.

Example:
The monster was frightened by Phyllis.

We can miss out the person who does the action:

The monster was frightened (<u>by Phyllis</u>).

We do this a lot in science:

The bunsen burner was lit (<u>by Shazia</u>).

See VOICE

Past participle   (1)

The past participle is a NON-FINITE part of the verb. It is used to form several TENSES.

Example:

The car was <u>stolen</u> from outside the house.

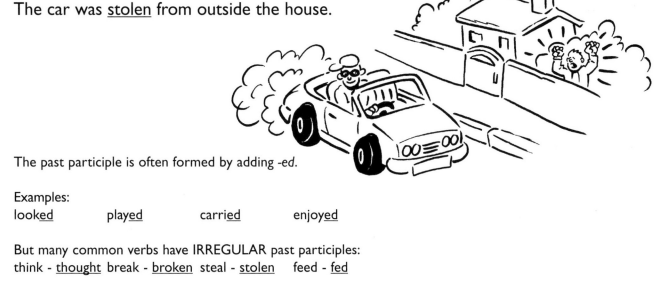

The past participle is often formed by adding -ed.

Examples:
look<u>ed</u>   play<u>ed</u>   carr<u>ied</u>   enjoy<u>ed</u>

But many common verbs have IRREGULAR past participles:
think - <u>thought</u> break - <u>broken</u> steal - <u>stolen</u>   feed - <u>fed</u>

Past participle (2)

The past participle can be used as an ADJECTIVE.

Example:

The <u>stolen</u> car was worth a lot of money.

Past participle (3)

We can use a past participle to join SENTENCES.

Example:

The thief got a lot of money for the car <u>stolen</u> from outside the house.

To join sentences in this way, we cut out the SUBJECT (<u>the car</u>) and the AUXILIARY VERB (<u>was</u>).

Example:
~~The car was~~ worth a lot of money.
The car was stolen from outside the house.

See MINOR CLAUSE

Past tense

A VERB in the past TENSE tells us that something happened in the past.

Example:

We <u>fed</u> the giraffes.

Perfect aspect

If a VERB is in the perfect ASPECT, the action is finished (at the time of speaking).

Examples:
He <u>has come</u> down the slide.   He <u>had cleaned</u> his shoes when the phone rang.

The perfect TENSES consist of :

to have	+	PAST PARTICIPLE	
has		washed	(present perfect tense)
had		cleaned	(past perfect tense)
will have		done	(future perfect tense)

Person

PRONOUNS are first, second or third person:

The *first person* is the speaker or writer:
I, me, we, us.

The *second person* is the person who is being spoken to:
you

The *third person* is whoever the speaker is talking about:
he, him, she, her, it, they, them.

See GENDER, NUMBER

Phrase

A phrase is a group of WORDS which act together as:

ADJECTIVE
The bicycle with bent handlebars.

ADVERB
He found seven baby rabbits in the hutch.

NOUN
The crazy old goalkeeper with the big white beard.

VERB
Jim should not have been kicking the ball

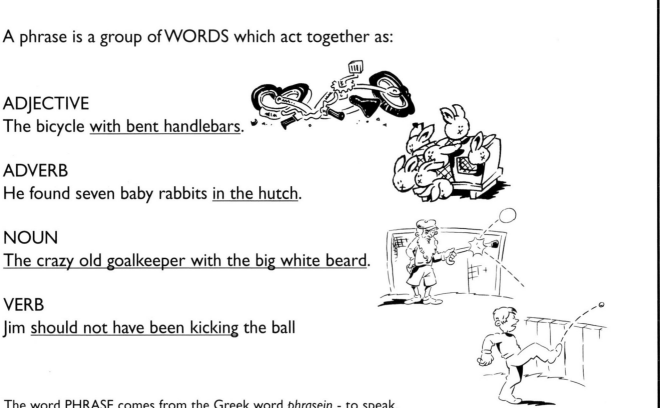

The word PHRASE comes from the Greek word *phrasein* - to speak.

Plural

Plural means more than one.

Examples:

frogs

children

Kinds of words which may be plural

NOUNS: dogs   the goals

PRONOUNS :   we   they   these   those

See NUMBER

Possessive

Possessive words tell us that something belongs to someone.

Examples:

It's mine!

Daisy's tractor

Happy Birthday Daisy

Kinds of words which show possession:

NOUNS: Daisy's bike   King Arthur's sword   the teachers' grief

ADJECTIVES: her bike   his sword   their grief

PRONOUNS: hers   his   theirs

See APOSTROPHE 1, GENITIVE CASE

Prefix

Prefixes are BOUND MORPHEMES which go at the beginning of a WORD.
They change the meaning of the word.
Example:

Some prefixes make the word NEGATIVE.
lock – <u>un</u>lock
honest – <u>dis</u>honest
sense – <u>non</u>sense

Other prefixes
re – adds the meaning *again*   She <u>re</u>-read the book.
sub – adds the meaning *under*   <u>sub</u>-marine
pre – adds the meaning *before*   <u>pre</u>-paid

super – adds the meaning *over*   <u>super</u>-man
post – adds the meaning *after*   <u>post</u>-dated

Preposition

A preposition is one of the PARTS OF SPEECH. It shows the position of things and people.

Examples:

The dog is <u>in</u> the kennel   <u>under</u> the kennel
<u>beside</u> the kennel
<u>on</u> the kennel

See ACCUSATIVE CASE

Present participle   (1)

The present participle is a NON-FINITE VERB. It is formed by adding *-ing*.

It is used to form some TENSES:

Examples:
He was <u>coming</u> down the slide.   The children are <u>playing</u> in the park.

The present participle is used to form tenses together with the AUXILIARY VERB *to be*.

It forms verbs in the IMPERFECT ASPECT.

Present participle   (2)

We can use the present participle as an ADJECTIVE.

Examples:

We've had a <u>tiring</u> day.   The princess had long <u>flowing</u> hair.
Jim bowed to the <u>cheering</u> crowds.

Present participle (3)

We can use the present participle to join sentences.

Examples:

The canary was singing sweetly.

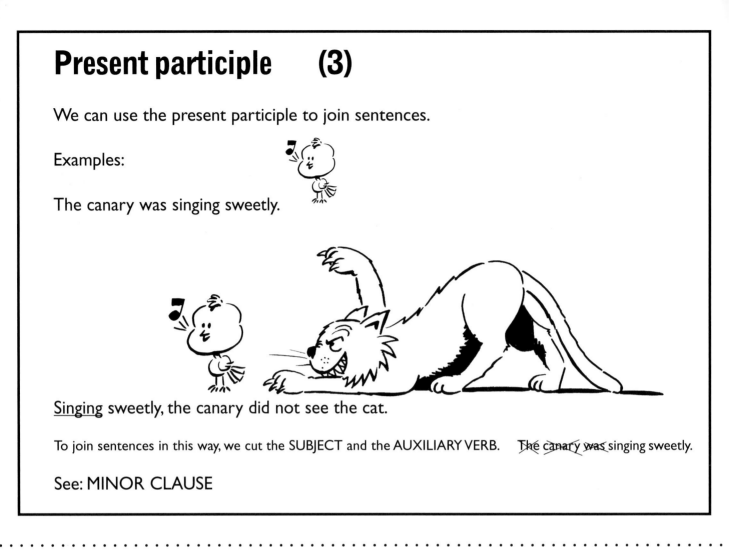

<u>Singing</u> sweetly, the canary did not see the cat.

To join sentences in this way, we cut the SUBJECT and the AUXILIARY VERB.   ~~The canary was~~ singing sweetly.

See: MINOR CLAUSE

Present tense

A VERB in the present TENSE tells us that it is happening now.

Examples:

We often <u>go</u> to bed late.
<u>Do</u> you <u>take</u> sugar?
They <u>are listening</u> to the news at the moment.

Pronoun

A pronoun is one of the PARTS OF SPEECH. It stands instead of a NOUN.

Examples:

Jude is always teasing his sisters . He is a nuisance and they are fed up with him.

Personal pronouns:	SINGULAR	PLURAL
First person:	*I, me*	*we, us*
Second person:	*you*	*you*
Third person:	*he, him*	*they, them*
	she, her, it	

Other kinds of pronouns: DEMONSTRATIVE, INTERROGATIVE, POSSESSIVE, RELATIVE

See PERSON, GENDER, NUMBER, CASE, PERSON

Question

When people want information they ask questions.

Example:

Has it shrunk?

In writing, a question ends with a QUESTION MARK.

WORD-ORDER:

VERB	SUBJECT	VERB
Has	it	shrunk?

See INTERROGATIVE , QUESTION MARK

Relative

Relative words link two CLAUSES.

Example:

Ahmed got the present <u>that</u> we gave him stuck in the door.

The word RELATIVE comes from the Latin *relatum – linked*.

Kinds of relative words:
PRONOUNS: <u>who </u>(for people), <u>which</u> (for things), <u>that</u> (for either)

ADVERBS: the place <u>where</u> she lives   the holiday <u>when</u> it rained all the time   the reason <u>why</u> he did it

. . . .

Semi-colon   ;   (1)

We use a semi-colon instead of a full stop when we want to show there is a connection between sentences.

Example:

The spider was behind the television; then it scuttled out and frightened us.

We have a choice about using a full stop or a semi-colon:

The spider was behind the television. Then it scuttled out and frightened us.

Sometimes we may feel like using a dash:

The spider was behind the television – then it scuttled out and frightened us.

Semi-colon ; (2)

We use semi-colons to mark off long items in a list.

Example:

Jim's mother was always complaining about him. For instance, he didn't wipe his feet when he came in from the garden; he refused to eat his greens; he didn't tidy his bedroom; and, to cap it all, he'd just lost his new gloves.

Sentence

We write in sentences.

Examples:

Once upon a time there was a king and a queen. They were very happy except for one thing. They had no children. Then at last they had a little girl, who would one day inherit the kingdom.

A sentence may consist of:

One CLAUSE: *Once upon a time there was a king and a queen.*
Or
More than one CLAUSE: *Then at last they had a little girl, who would day inherit the kingdom.*

A sentence begins with a CAPITAL LETTER (1) and ends with a FULL STOP (1).

See SIMPLE SENTENCE, COMPOUND SENTENCE, COMPLEX SENTENCE

Sentence adverb

These are WORDS which comment on the whole SENTENCE.

Example:

First of all, Joan suggested that the
creature lived in a burrow. Jitpu, as
usual, was sure that his aunt
had brought it back from India. Finally,
we decided that it must have come
from Outer Space. The creature,
however, sat there unmoved.

Sentence adverbs are not JOINING-WORDS.

If the sentence is short, we have the choice of using commas or not.
Example: First of all Joan suggested that the creature lived in a burrow.

See: COMMA (4)

Simple sentence

A simple sentence consists of one CLAUSE.

Examples:

Jim loves rabbits.

We gave Ahmed a present.

Charlene is an acrobat.

Singular

Singular means one person or thing - not many.

Examples:

a child

a frog

Kinds of words which may be singular:

NOUNS
Examples: the ball, a boy

PRONOUNS
Examples: I, me, he, him, this

See NUMBER

Speech marks "..."

We use speech marks to show that we are quoting the exact words which someone spoke. We use them a lot when we write stories.

"There's a funny sort of light in the sky," said Bernard. "It's getting nearer."
"Whatever can it be?" Shazia wondered.
"I don't know," said Felicity, "but I'm off!"

See QUOTATION MARKS

Statement

A statement is the kind of SENTENCE that gives information.

Example:

The rats are eating the electric cables.

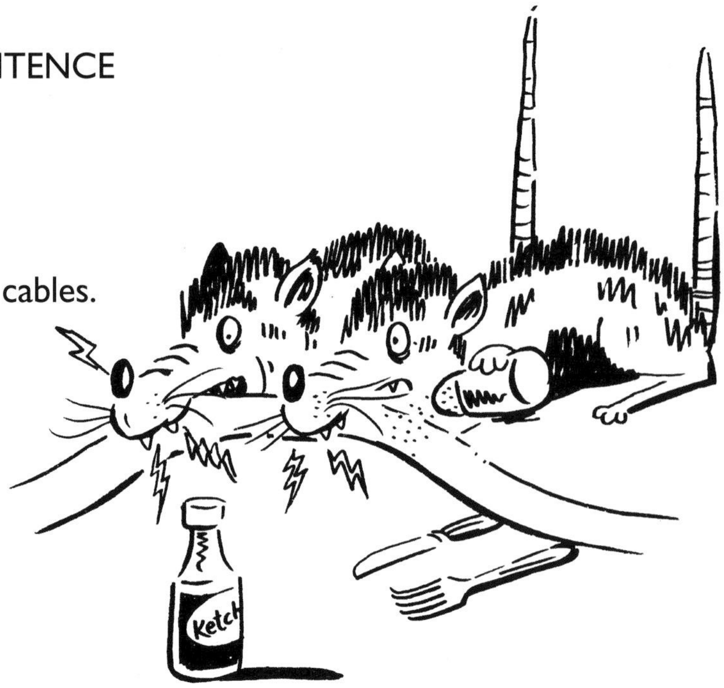

The VERB in a statement is in the DECLARATIVE MOOD.

See COMMAND, QUESTION

Subject

The subject is what we are talking about.

Examples:

<u>Jim</u> had not realised that <u>Floppy</u> was pregnant until <u>he</u> found seven baby rabbits in the hutch.

What can act as subject:

NOUN: <u>Floppy</u> was pregnant.
PRONOUN: <u>He</u> had not realised.
NOUN PHRASE: <u>The white rabbit with black spots</u> was his favourite.
NOUN CLAUSE: <u>What Jim did not know about rabbits</u> would fill a book.

WORD-ORDER: The subject comes in first place before the verb: SUBJECT   VERB
                                                                     <u>Jim</u>   had not realised

See NOMINATIVE CASE

Subordinate clause

A subordinate clause is a CLAUSE which cannot
stand alone.

Examples:

Ahmed got the present <u>that we gave him</u> stuck in the door.

Jim had not known <u>that Floppy was pregnant</u> .
Jim passed the ball to Harriet, <u>if he could.</u>

A subordinate clause is linked to a MAIN
CLAUSE and forms part of a COMPLEX SENTENCE.

Kinds of subordinate clause: ADJECTIVE CLAUSE, ADVERB CLAUSE, NOUN CLAUSE

Suffix

Suffixes are BOUND MORPHEMES which we add to the end of WORDS.
They change the grammar of the word.

Examples:

hard-<u>er</u>   dress-<u>ed</u>   entertain-<u>ment</u>   grow-<u>ing</u>
elephant-<u>s</u>   goalkeep-<u>er</u>

Some examples:
-<u>er</u> makes the COMPARATIVE
I work hard.
He works hard-<u>er</u>.

-<u>ed</u> makes the PAST TENSE
I play.   *I play-<u>ed</u>.*

-<u>ment</u> makes a VERB into a NOUN
He entertained us.
We enjoyed the entertain<u>ment</u>.

-<u>s</u> makes SINGULAR nouns
PLURAL
I have one rabbit.
She has several rabbit-<u>s</u>.

See PREFIX

Superlative

The superlative tells who or what is the biggest, smallest, fastest, slowest etc.

Example:

Rashida is a fast runner.   Harry is a faster runner.   Germaine is <u>the fastest</u> runner.

The Guinness Book of Records is full of superlatives.

See COMPARATIVE

Kinds of WORDS which have a superlative form
ADJECTIVES: *the deepest river*
the most horrible sight
ADVERBS: *She can throw <u>the farthest</u>.*
This rabbit escapes <u>the most often</u>.

Tense

The tense of a VERB tells us whether something happens in the present, the past or the future.

Examples:

FUTURE TENSE
Sharon <u>will surf</u> at the beach tomorrow morning.

PRESENT TENSE
Sharon <u>is surfing</u> at the   beach this morning.

PAST TENSE
Sharon <u>surfed</u> at the beach this morning.

See AUXILIARY, PAST PARTICIPLE (1), PRESENT PARTICIPLE (1)

Transitive verb

A transitive verb has an OBJECT.

Example:

SUBJECT	VERB	OBJECT
The children	rang	the alarm.

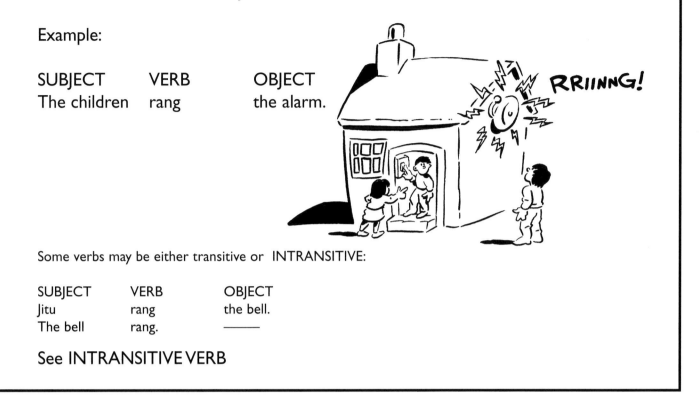

RRIInnG!

Some verbs may be either transitive or INTRANSITIVE:

SUBJECT	VERB	OBJECT
Jitu	rang	the bell.
The bell	rang.	———

See INTRANSITIVE VERB

Verb

The verb is one of the PARTS OF SPEECH. It is the most important WORD in the CLAUSE. It tells us what happens.

NOUNS name things, but without a verb they do not make sense.

Examples: 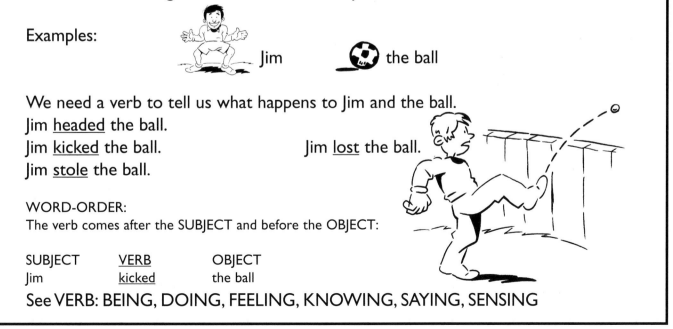 Jim   the ball

We need a verb to tell us what happens to Jim and the ball.
Jim <u>headed</u> the ball.
Jim <u>kicked</u> the ball.   Jim <u>lost</u> the ball.
Jim <u>stole</u> the ball.

WORD-ORDER:
The verb comes after the SUBJECT and before the OBJECT:

SUBJECT	<u>VERB</u>	OBJECT
Jim	<u>kicked</u>	the ball

See VERB: BEING, DOING, FEELING, KNOWING, SAYING, SENSING

Verb: being

Some VERBS say what things <u>are</u>.

Examples:

She <u>is</u> a carpenter.

He <u>has become</u> a very nice person
The old lady <u>looked</u> lonely.

These verbs are followed by a COMPLEMENT.

Verb: doing

Most VERBS are doing-words.

Examples:

Jim <u>lost</u> the ball.

Jim <u>headed</u> the ball.
Jim <u>stole</u> the ball.
Jim <u>kicked</u> the ball.

Verb: feeling

Some VERBS say how we feel.

Examples:

She <u>fears</u> spiders.

He <u>loves</u> basketball.
Uncle John <u>hated</u> Aunt Mary's puddings.
We <u>enjoy</u> cycling.

Verb: knowing

Some VERBS say what is happening in our heads.

Examples:

She <u>was dreaming</u> of going abroad.

We <u>didn't understand</u> the question.
I <u>wondered</u> what to do next.

Verb: saying

Some VERBS tell what we say.

Examples: She <u>screamed</u> at me.

I <u>told</u> him to be careful.
No-one <u>laughed</u> at the joke.
You<u>'re muttering</u> again!

Verb: sensing

Verbs say what we do with our senses.

Examples: The monster <u>saw</u> us.

We <u>could</u> <u>hear</u> footsteps.
Can you <u>smell</u> burning?
<u>Feel</u> this velvet!

Verb phrase

A verb phrase is a VERB which consists of two or more WORDS.

Examples:

Jim <u>will kick</u> the ball.

Jim <u>must have kicked</u> the ball.

<u>Might</u> Jim <u>be kicking</u> the ball?

Jim <u>has not been kicking</u> the ball.

Jim <u>should not have been kicking</u> the ball.

See AUXILIARY VERB, MODAL VERB, ASPECT, TENSE, VOICE, NEGATIVE,

Voice

This is the choice between ACTIVE and PASSIVE.

ACTIVE:
Phyllis frightened the monster.

PASSIVE:
The monster was frightened by Phyllis.

WORD-ORDER:	SUBJECT	VERB	OBJECT	ADVERB
ACTIVE	Phyllis	frightened	the monster	
PASSIVE	The monster	was frightened		by Phyllis

Word

A word is the smallest piece of language which can stand alone.

Examples:

cables   rats   electric   the   chewed

We use grammar to combine words to make sense.

The rats chewed the electric cables.

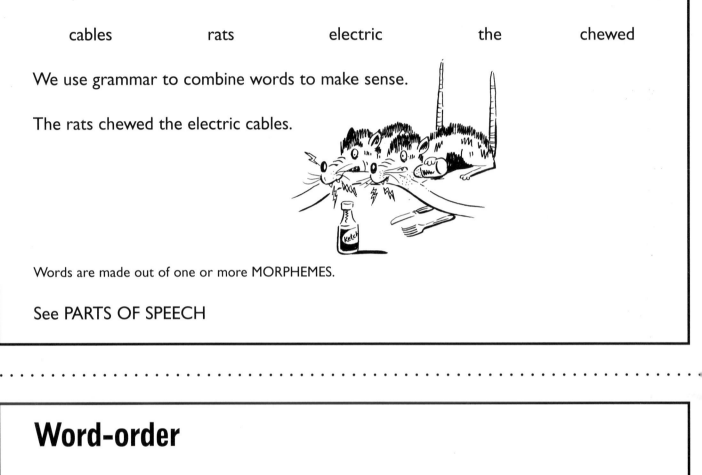

Words are made out of one or more MORPHEMES.

See PARTS OF SPEECH

Word-order

The word-order shows the work which WORDS do in a CLAUSE.

Example:

SUBJECT	VERB	OBJECT		SUBJECT	VERB	OBJECT
The tiger	killed	the farmer.		The farmer	killed	the tiger.

The words in these sentences are the same. Only the word-order shows us who got killed.

Word-order is very important in English. Some languages use CASE to show the work which words do.

See ADJECTIVE, ADVERB, ARTICLE, ADVERB CLAUSE, INTERROGATIVE (1) and (2), OBJECT, SUBJECT